AUSTRALIA'S REMARKABLE WILDLIFE

JOHN LESLEY

KANGAROO

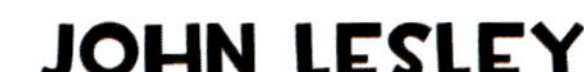

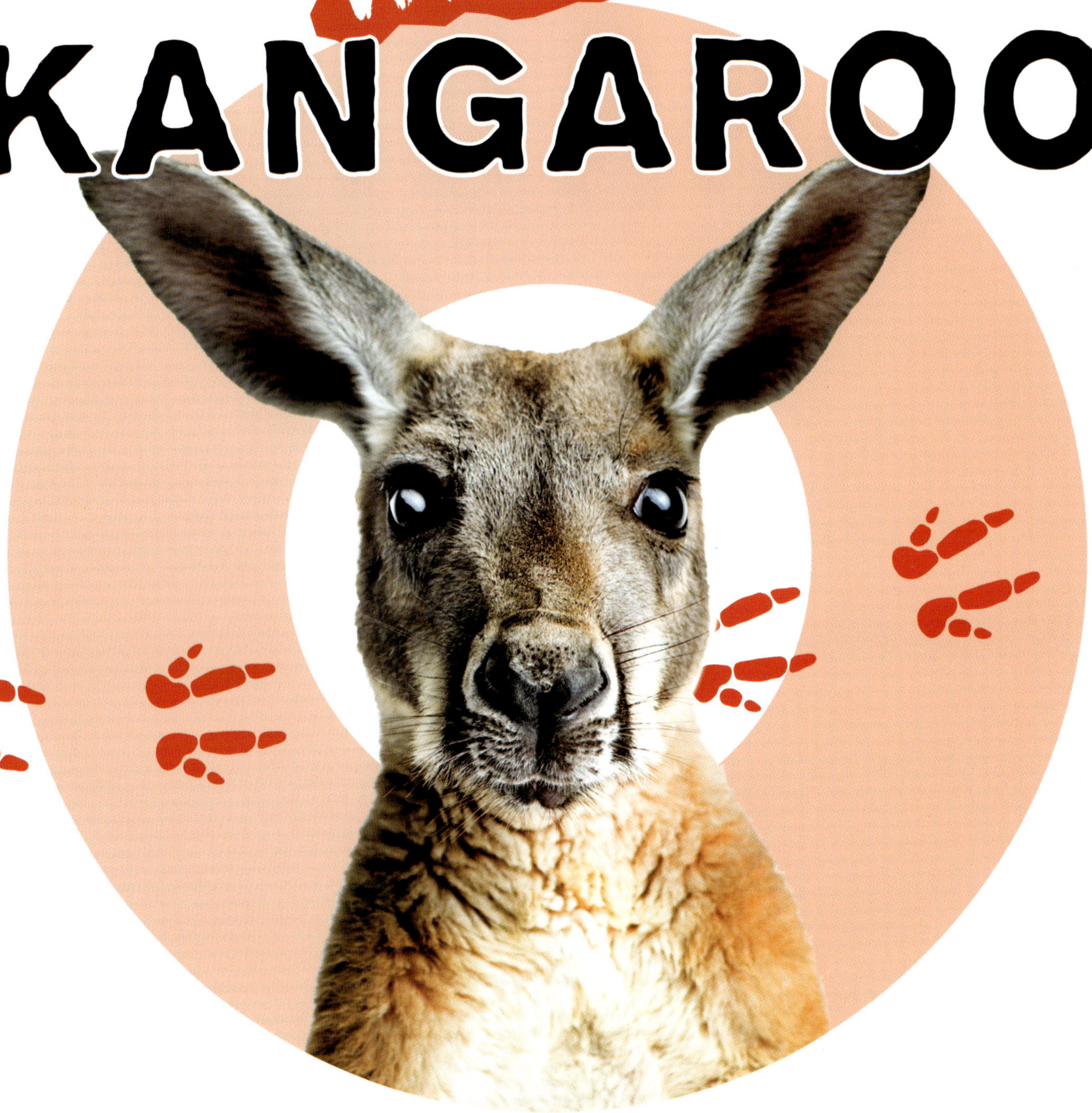

REDBACK publishing

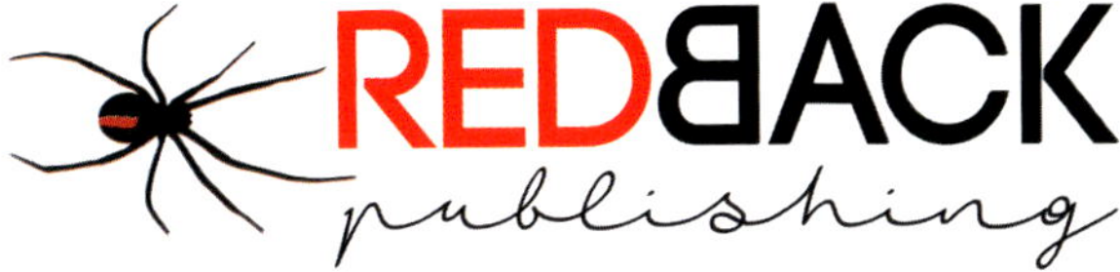

First Published 2022 by
Redback Publishing
PO Box 357 Frenchs Forest NSW 2086
Australia

www.redbackpublishing.com
orders@redbackpublishing.com

ISBN 978-1-925860-97-9

Author: John Lesley
Editor: Caroline Thomas
Design: Redback Publishing

NATIONAL LIBRARY OF AUSTRALIA

A catalogue record for this book is available from the National Library of Australia

Originated by Redback Publishing

Printed and bound in Malaysia.

Acknowledgements
Abbreviations: l—left, r—right, b—bottom, t—top, c—centre, m—middle
We would like to thank the following for permission to reproduce photographs: (Images © shutterstock) p11tr ChameleonsEye, p11bm Nobu Tamura via Wikimedia Commons, p26cm NextNewMedia.

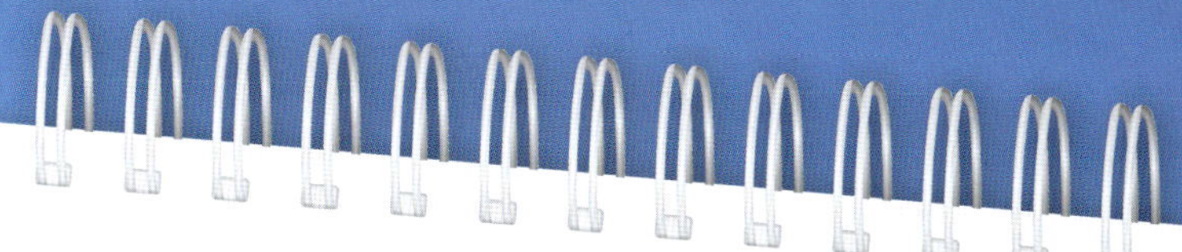

CONTENTS

KANGAROO BASIC FACTS

SCIENTIFIC NAME

Macropus. This Latin word means 'having long feet'.

TYPE OF ANIMAL

Marsupial mammal.

SIZE

Red kangaroos can grow to 2 metres tall and weigh over 80 kilograms. Other types of kangaroos, such as the black wallaroo, are much smaller.

COLOUR

The fur of kangaroos can be red, grey or brown, depending on the species.

CONSERVATION STATUS

Red and grey kangaroos are very common and not under threat of extinction. Some of the smaller and rarer kangaroos need to live in protected habitats to survive.

KANGAROO MOBS

A group of kangaroos is called a mob. A mob of kangaroos all hopping at top speed across open grasslands is an impressive sight. Some mobs can have hundreds of kangaroos in them.

A mob of kangaroos

Each mob has one dominant male

HOPPING

The distinctive feature of the kangaroo is that it hops. A large kangaroo has enormous strength in its back legs and can cover many metres in one hop.

They use much less energy than people do when they try to hop. Because of this, the big red and grey kangaroos have evolved to live in open grassland, where they can cover long distances easily.

The ability to hop while not using a lot of energy lets kangaroos survive in semi-desert areas, where water sources are very far apart.

Jumping over 7 metres in just one hop is easy for the biggest kangaroos because the tendons in their hind legs act like springs. Red kangaroos can hop as fast as a horse can gallop.

THE KANGAROO'S TAIL

The long, muscular tail is important for helping a kangaroo to keep its balance, both when it is sitting still and when it is hopping along quickly.

Kangaroos are clumsy walkers. When moving slowly, such as when they are grazing, they move forward by pushing against the ground with their tail.

Grazing kangaroos balance on their tail

Kangaroos use their tails for balance when hopping

4K UHD 3...2...1......1...2...3 00:35:02

KANGAROO PAWS

A kangaroo's front paws are very small compared to its back legs.

The front paws have a number of uses:

They are used to steady the kangaroo when it is standing still.

The claws are useful for grooming the fur.

Kangaroos dig with their front claws when searching for grass roots to eat or for water.

Fighting kangaroos try to scratch each other with the claws on their front paws.

Newborn joeys climb across the mother's fur to her pouch using their front paws.

Kangaroos often dig a shallow hole to sit in during the heat of the day.

Kangaroo paw

WALLABY OR KANGAROO?

WHAT'S THE DIFFERENCE?

Wallabies and kangaroos are very similar, except that wallabies are smaller. They both belong to the animal group called *Macropus*.

Wallabies live in different habitats from kangaroos. Since they are smaller, wallabies can live on more hilly landscapes and in thicker bushland. They can even live in mountainous and rocky areas.

Wallabies and kangaroos are different species, which means that they do not breed together.

Rock wallaby with a joey

KANGAROO FOSSILS

Kangaroos first appeared on Earth millions of years ago. Their ancestors lived in trees, but evolved adaptations that enabled them to hop on the ground.

A large kangaroo that weighed hundreds of kilograms only became extinct about 15,000 years ago. Aboriginal people would have known about the monster kangaroo, which scientists now call *Procoptodon*.

Thousands of years ago, a meat-eating kangaroo lived in Australia. It stood two metres tall and may have held its prey with its front paws.

TYPES OF KANGAROOS

WESTERN GREY KANGAROO

The western grey kangaroo has brown or grey fur.

RED KANGAROO

The red kangaroo lives in the semi-arid grasslands of inland Australia. They are the biggest of all the kangaroos, and also the largest marsupials in the world.

Red kangaroo

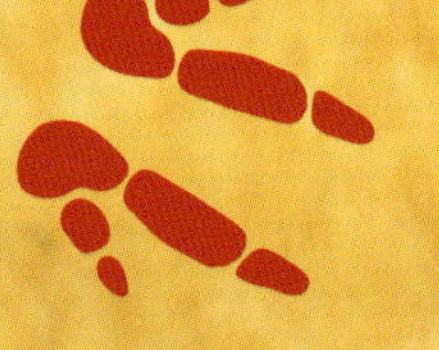

EASTERN GREY KANGAROO

The eastern grey kangaroo lives in open forests, but is also often seen on farmland, eating grass alongside sheep or cattle.

Eastern grey kangaroos

Western grey kangaroos

Common wallaroo

WALLAROO

A wallaroo is midway in size between a kangaroo and a wallaby. There are a few different types of wallaroo, but the 'common wallaroo' is the one that is most often seen. Wallaroos live in a variety of habitats, from rocky hills to bushland and grassy areas.

TREE KANGAROOS

We are used to seeing kangaroos hopping across the outback of Australia, but some species have a completely different lifestyle. They live in trees!

Tree kangaroos live in tropical rainforests in Papua New Guinea, Indonesia and in the north of Australia. On the forest floor they hop, but their back legs and front paws are both also adapted for holding on when climbing.

Baby tree kangaroo

Tree kangaroos are a threatened species due to the ongoing loss of their rainforest habitat.

KEEPING COOL

Kangaroos live in some of the hottest habitats in Australia. They keep cool by sitting in the shade, and by licking their front paws. As the saliva dries, it cools down the body.

Kangaroos licking their paws to keep cool

Kangaroo lying in the shade

BABY KANGAROOS

LIFE CYCLE

A baby kangaroos is called a joey. It is born as a tiny, underdeveloped baby that has to crawl across its mother's fur to reach her pouch. Once inside, the hairless, pink joey attaches itself to a teat and feeds on milk.

A kangaroo can live for about five years in the wild, but may live to twenty years old in a zoo.

Only the female kangaroo has a pouch.

FOOD

Kangaroos mainly eat grass and leaves. In dry regions, they use their front paws to dig into the ground to find water.

Predators of kangaroos include dogs and dingoes. Younger joeys are the preferred prey, as large adults can be aggressive and will fight off most attacks.

In Australia, people can only hunt and kill kangaroos under strict conditions. They can be killed to legally reduce their numbers, for the legal sale of their meat, or for traditional uses by Indigenous Australians.

SWIMMING

Kangaroos can swim and may jump into water to escape predators such as dogs, dingoes or people.

People have seen kangaroos swimming in all sorts of locations, including rivers, lakes, the ocean surf and even when they fall into swimming pools.

Lucky Bay, Western Australia

In true Australian fashion, they love a day spent lazing on the sand at a beach, followed by a dip in the water.

Jervis Bay in New South Wales and Lucky Bay in Western Australia are just two places where kangaroos enjoy the beach.

HOW DO THEY COMMUNICATE?

Kangaroos communicate with each other by sound, smell and behaviour.

Female kangaroos make noises to their joeys.

Male kangaroos make grunting, hissing or growling noises.

Some kangaroos thump the ground with their feet to warn of danger.

Male kangaroos use smell to let others know they are around. They leave their smell in an area using urine or by rubbing a gland on the front of their chest onto grass or trees.

When male kangaroos fight, they stand up on their hind legs.

WHERE TO SEE A KANGAROO

KANGAROOS IN ZOOS

Members of the ordinary public are not allowed to keep a kangaroo as a pet. Zoos, animal carers and wildlife parks need to obtain special permission before they can keep kangaroos. Many wildlife parks in Australia allow visitors to feed and pat their kangaroos.

IN THE WILD

The larger types of kangaroos are not rare, and it is common to see one or even a whole mob when driving in country areas.

TAKE CARE WHEN DRIVING

Kangaroos have a habit of running directly in front of a car, rather than away from it. This is a protective reaction to being chased by a predator, where suddenly changing direction creates confusion. A car does not react in the same way a dog would and the kangaroo sadly becomes a casualty as a result.

PEOPLE AND KANGAROOS

GRAZING

Kangaroos graze on the same grasslands where farmers keep sheep and cattle. In times of drought, there is competition for the grass and water supply.

INJURED KANGAROOS

If you find an injured kangaroo by the side of a road, contact a wildlife rescue service. If the kangaroo is dead and it is a female, check if it has a live joey in its pouch and report this as well.

Rescued joey being fed milk

4K UHD 3...2...1...0...1...2...3 00:35:02

KANGAROOS AS PETS? NO!

It is illegal in Australia to keep a kangaroo as a pet.

BOXING KANGAROOS

Kangaroos fight each other by kicking with their hind legs and hitting with their front paws. In the past, people used this behaviour to put kangaroos in boxing fights with humans. Thankfully, this awful activity is now illegal.

KANGAROO STEAKS

Kangaroos have been used as a source of meat for thousands of years by the Indigenous people of Australia. Kangaroo meat is now served in restaurants around Australia and is exported as well. Pet food sold in stores often contains kangaroo meat.

Kangaroos are not suitable for farming, so the meat comes from the killing of wild animals. Only licensed hunters are permitted to hunt kangaroos. Anyone else who harms a kangaroo will face severe legal penalties.

neck
saddle
forequarters
leg
tail
shank

THREATS TO KANGAROOS

Hunting by humans

Attacks by feral dogs and dingoes

Rescued joey in a makeshift pouch

Lack of water during drought

Kangaroo habitat is cleared for farmland

Loss of habitat and food sources

THE FUTURE OF KANGAROOS

In 2018, images of a wallaby hopping across the Sydney Harbour Bridge amused people all over the world. This rare event was actually a little sad, since it meant that a wild creature had lost its way in a big city.

As cities expand further into bushland, kangaroos will lose more of their habitats. In the semi-arid parts of central Australia, kangaroo habitats are less under threat, and they will continue to live a natural existence for a long time into the future.

SYMBOLS OF AUSTRALIA

The Australian Boomers men's basketball team is named after a male kangaroo, which is called a boomer.

The kangaroo is one of the animals holding up the shield on the Australian coat-of-arms.

The Australian airline, Qantas, uses the red kangaroo as its logo.

Skippy was a television star during the 1960s. Famous worldwide for his adventures, Skippy's skills were more than a little beyond the capabilities of any real-life kangaroo.

At the 2000 Olympic Games opening ceremony, Australian athletes carried a boxing kangaroo toy, symbolising their competitive spirit.

Tourism Australia uses a colourful, hopping kangaroo as its logo.

The Australian Made logo has a yellow kangaroo outline on a green background. It shows that a product was made in Australia.

SORTING ANIMALS INTO GROUPS

Biologists divide all living things around the world into groups. They call this process classification.

Here are the basic groups that describe all animals with backbones:

AMPHIBIANS

Examples include frogs and salamanders. Amphibians start life in water but later grow lungs so they can breathe air on land.

MAMMALS

Examples include dingoes and possums. Mammals are warm-blooded, have fur and feed their young on milk.

FISH

Examples include sharks and goldfish.

BIRDS

Examples include emus and penguins. Birds are the only animals with feathers.

REPTILES

Examples include lizards and snakes. Reptiles are cold-blooded and are covered in scales.

Mammals are further divided into three main groups:

MONOTREME MAMMALS

Examples include echidnas and platypuses. Monotreme mammals lay eggs.

MARSUPIAL MAMMALS

Examples include kangaroos and koalas. Marsupial mammals produce tiny, underdeveloped babies that continue to grow inside their parent's pouch.

PLACENTAL MAMMALS

Examples include whales and humans. Placental mammals have or once had fur, and they grow their babies inside their bodies.

Humans have a scientific name and a position in the classification of animals. We are called *Homo sapiens*. These Latin words mean 'smart person'.

GLOSSARY

adaptation feature of a living thing that allows it to survive in its environment

biologist scientist who studies living things

dominant more powerful than others

habitat normal place in the wild where an animal lives

joey baby marsupial

Latin language used by the ancient Romans and still used for some scientific purposes

mammal animal that is warm-blooded, has fur and feeds its babies with milk

marsupial type of mammal with a pouch for its babies

mob group of kangaroos

outback remote, country areas of Australia

prey animal that another animal eats

semi-arid area with low rainfall and little water

species different types of animals

teat nipple from which a baby animal drinks milk

tendon substance that attaches muscles to bones

INDEX